Johnson's®

potty training

DK Publishing Inc

London, New York, Munich, Melbourne, Delhi

Text by Tracey Godridge

For Cora, Eden, and Noah

Senior editors Julia North, Salima Hirani
U.S. Senior editor Jennifer Williams
Senior art editor Hannah Moore
Project editor Angela Baynham
Project art editor Alison Turner
DTP designer Karen Constanti
Production controller Heather Hughes
Managing editors Anna Davidson, Liz Coghill
Managing art editor Glenda Fisher
Photography art direction Sally Smallwood
Photography Ruth Jenkinson
Americanizer Christine Heilman
Proofreader Cari Luna

Publishing director Corinne Roberts

First American Edition, 2004
This edition published 2006
Published in the United States by
DK Publishing, Inc., 375 Hudson Street,
New York, New York 10014

06 07 08 10 9 8 7 6 5 4 3 2

Book title JOHNSON'S® *Potty Training*
copyright © Johnson & Johnson, Ltd. 2004, 2006

Cover design copyright © Johnson & Johnson, Ltd.
and Dorling Kindersley, Ltd. 2004, 2006

Text copyright © Dorling Kindersley, Ltd. 2004, 2006

Images copyright © Dorling Kindersley, Ltd. 2004, 2006

JOHNSON'S® is a registered trademark of Johnson & Johnson

A Cataloging-in-Publication record for this book is available from the Library of Congress.

ISBN 0-7566-1779-0

Reproduced by Colourscan, Singapore
Printed in Singapore by Star Standard Industries (PTE) Ltd

Discover more at
www.dk.com

A message to parents from
Johnson's®

The most precious gift in the world is a new baby. To your little one, you are the center of the universe. And by following your most basic instincts to touch, hold, and talk to your baby, you provide the best start to a happy, healthy life.

Our baby products encourage parents to care for and nurture their children through the importance of touch, developing a deep, loving bond that transcends all others.

Parenting is not an exact science, nor is it a one-size-fits-all formula. For more than a hundred years, Johnson & Johnson has supported the healthcare needs of parents and healthcare professionals, and we understand that all parents feel more confident in their role when they have information they can trust.

That is why we offer this book as our commitment to you to provide scientifically sound, professionally reviewed guidance on the important topics of pregnancy, baby care, and child development.

As you read through this book, the most important thing to remember is this: you know your baby better than anyone else. By watching, listening, and having confidence in your natural ability, you will know how to use the information you have in your hands, for the benefit of the baby in your arms.

Contents

1 Your toddler's development **6**

2 Preparing your toddler **16**

3 First days out of diapers **26**

4 What to expect **36**

5 Out and about **46**

6 Dry at night **52**

Potty training guide **60**

Useful contacts **62**

Index **63**

Acknowledgments **64**

" I didn't even **start to think** about potty training until my son was two-and-a-half. Then, once we took the plunge, he was **dry in days.** "

ELIZABETH, mother of Max, age three

Your toddler's development

You know your toddler is growing up when she makes the big step out of diapers into underpants. But this won't happen until her brain is developed enough to control her bowel and bladder—at any time between 18 and 36 months—and she has reached a certain level of emotional and physical maturity.

The physical basics

You probably can hardly wait to introduce your toddler to the potty, especially after months of diaper-changing. A life without diapers will be lighter on your workload as well as on your checkbook! But until she's physically and emotionally ready, there's nothing you can do to speed up the process.

Until now, your toddler has emptied her bladder and bowel automatically as a reflex action whenever they felt full. She will begin to be aware that she's peeing or pooping only when the nerve pathways from her bladder and bowel to her brain have fully matured. This usually happens at around 18 months of age.

Even then, she still won't be able to predict when she needs to empty her bowels and bladder—it will be some time before she's familiar with the feelings of needing to go and has developed the physical control to hold it. This usually happens by about two-and-a-half years, although it can be earlier or later.

Mastering new skills

Gaining a sense of bowel and bladder control is an exciting step forward. But your toddler also needs to be willing and able to cope with the mechanics of using a potty. As with all new skills, your toddler will master potty training in her own way and at her own speed. Some toddlers—usually the older ones—become potty-trained very quickly and rarely have an accident, while the majority have false starts and setbacks along the way.

Getting ready

Your toddler needs a variety of physical, verbal, and emotional skills before she's ready for potty training.
• **Ability to "hold it"** If your child

Expert tip

Potty training has a strong genetic component. So if you want clues to when your child is likely to be ready, it may be worth asking your parents about your own performance as a toddler.

is managing a reasonable amount of time during the day without peeing, then she is probably developing some control over her bladder. Potty training isn't really practical if she's wetting her diaper every hour or so. You can check to see how frequently she's peeing by checking her diaper. If it's still dry after a couple of hours, that's a good first step.
• **Awareness of what she's doing** Watch her face—she may stop playing, stand still, look at you, get red in the face, and even try to tell you what's happening.

Is my toddler ready for potty training?

Only your toddler can tell you whether or not she's ready for potty training. She won't use words—but watch her closely and you should be able to spot the telltale signs. Lots of toddlers reach this stage sometime between 18 and 24 months—but many others aren't ready until some months later.

Spotting the signs

You'll be thinking about potty training some time around your toddler's second birthday. But is she thinking about it, too? There are many different signs that your child may be ready to start—here's a checklist to help you figure out whether or not now is a good time to get started:

★ your child stays dry for at least two hours at a time during the day or is dry after naps

★ her bowel movements are fairly regular

★ her diaper is often dry—this shows she can go for a while without peeing

★ she's aware when she's peeing or pooping

★ she's reasonably coordinated and can sit comfortably on the potty and pull her pants up and down

★ she's interested in what happens when you use the toilet.

"WHAT ARE YOU DOING, MOM?"
If your child seems interested in what's going on when you use the toilet, this is a good sign that she will be ready to start potty training soon.

A NEED FOR INDEPENDENCE
As your little one gets older, she will want more independence. If she's trying to do things such as putting her coat on by herself, you can start thinking about potty training.

FOLLOWING INSTRUCTIONS
Being able to follow simple instructions—passing you something when you ask her to, for example—is another sign that your child is ready for potty training.

Other signs of nearing readiness:
★ she can follow simple instructions
★ she's eager to do things for herself
★ she's eager to please and imitate you
★ she shows a desire for independence.
You don't need to be able to check off every item in this list to start potty training, but before you take the plunge, your toddler should know when she's pooping or peeing, and show an interest in being "like a grownup."

Your toddler is not ready if:
★ she's under 18 months old
★ she has no idea what's happening when she pees or poops
★ she isn't interested in imitating you
★ she's resistant to being told what to do.

Expert tips

Even if your toddler isn't ready to start using a potty, it's worth introducing the subject in a low-key way:

• when you change her diaper, use words such as "poop" and "pee"

• stay matter-of-fact—not critical—about the state of her diapers

• discourage older children from making any negative comments about dirty diapers

• let her see you using the toilet.

When Alex was about two-and-a-half, he started to become aware of when he was peeing or pooping and would often come and tell me. I quickly realized the time had arrived when he was ready to take the big step from diapers to underpants.

SUZANNE, mother of Alex, age three

If she has no clothes on and is looking at the puddle she made and clutching herself, then she's also connecting the feeling she has with what has happened.

• **Coordination** Very young children and those who were slower learning to crawl and walk may have problems getting on and off the potty. Pulling their pants up and down may be tricky for them, too. Knocking over a potty or struggling with clothes will inevitably be upsetting for your child and frustrating for you.

• **Understanding of what you tell her** By two years old, most toddlers are saying their first words, and they may have the words "poop" or "pee" (or whichever you choose to use) already in their vocabulary. Even if your toddler isn't talking much yet, it's a huge help if she can understand what you are saying when, for example, you show her a potty and explain what it's for. Being able to follow simple instructions such as "let's find your potty" will also help her grasp what's needed and when.

DIAPER CHECK
Noting how often your child's diaper is wet will give you some idea of when she's ready to start potty training.

Questions & Answers

Do boys take longer than girls?
Lots of moms say that their daughters were out of diapers earlier than their sons—and, on the whole, girls do seem to master potty training before boys. Boys, for example, appear to be less interested than girls at the same age, and tend to have accidents up to a later age than girls. This could be related to their language skills—girls are often more eager to communicate at this age, and success at potty training depends to a certain extent on understanding language and being able to respond to it. Potty training isn't a race—and it's worth remembering that the toddler who starts later often gets there faster!

My mother says I was potty-trained by 18 months. Could this be true?
In the days before disposables, when diapers were washed by hand, moms were eager to get their toddlers "dry" as quickly as possible. However, it's likely it had more to do with good timing than training. Figuring out when your child is likely to poop—after a meal, for example—and then sitting her on the potty until she does may teach her what her potty is for, but not how to control her bowel movements. True potty training is when you give your toddler the chance to recognize for herself when she needs to empty her bowel or bladder—and she can only do this when she is developmentally ready.

● **Willingness to try** At around 18 months, when toddlers experience a surge of independence, difficult behavior is common. Refusing to cooperate in even the simplest task is entirely normal for a child this age. Coping with resistance from your toddler can be challenging at the best of times. Instead of putting your toddler—or yourself—under any extra pressure, wait for a time when she's feeling less negative.

Making the right decision
Social pressure to potty-train your toddler before she's ready can be intense. Maybe your friend's son is the same age and is out of diapers already and you're worried that your daughter should be, too. Perhaps you're expecting another

STAY POSITIVE
Avoid negative comments about the state of your child's diapers when you change them.

SUMMER FUN
*Warm, sunny days provide a great opportunity for your child
to get used to spending time without her diaper.*

Children with special needs

Mastering potty training is a major
achievement for all children—and
those with special needs especially
benefit from this step toward
independence. It can, however,
take a lot longer for a child with
physical or learning difficulties,
and will certainly involve a much
greater degree of patience and
understanding. Children who have
hearing problems, for example,
will find communication harder;
those with coordination problems
will find coping with clothes and
sitting on a potty difficult.

If your child has special needs,
you may find expert help useful in
judging the right time to start and
the best way of teaching bowel and
bladder control. Support groups can
offer useful information on this
subject and will be able to put you
in touch with other parents who
can share their experiences with
you. Your healthcare provider is also
a good starting point.

baby and feel life with a newborn
would be easier if your oldest child
was out of diapers. Or maybe your
parents are making you feel guilty
that your child isn't potty-trained
yet—40 years ago, early potty
training was much more popular.

When it comes to giving up
diapers, however, there's only one
timetable that matters to your
toddler, and that's her own. Try to
remember that your toddler has a
better chance of success if you wait
until she's clearly ready. Meanwhile,

explain to friends and family the approach you are taking and ask for their support.

Going at her pace

There's little point in trying to potty-train your toddler before she has reached the required stages of development (see pages 8–9). Starting too soon will, at best, result in lots of puddles and soiled clothes; at worst, your toddler will become upset and possibly resistant; and the whole process will take a lot longer.

Like crawling and walking, potty training is a developmental task that your toddler will prepare for at her own pace. And whether she gets there earlier or later has no connection with her intelligence or other areas of development. For example, a child who was slow to crawl won't necessarily be older when she's ready for potty training; and similarly, a child who is out of diapers at a younger age won't necessarily be an early reader.

The best route to success is to follow your child's lead. After all, there's no hurry—and, as with acquiring all new skills, your toddler will get there in her own time. Being patient and waiting for signs of readiness and willingness helps pave the way for earlier success—which, in turn, will give your toddler a real confidence boost.

Potty training twins

If you are the parent of twins—and dealing with a double load of diapers—there may be an extra temptation to rush potty training. As with singletons, however, starting your twin toddlers before they are ready could backfire. Coping with double the number of wet pants and puddles can't be any better than changing extra diapers.

It's possible that one of your twins will be ready before the other, since all children—even twins—develop at different rates. Seeing a sibling's progress may spur the other one along in the right direction. But don't forget that potty training isn't a competition—either between the children in your family or between peers. If one toddler is interested before the other, try to encourage and praise in a low-key way. Even if your other twin appears to be totally uninterested, hearing her brother or sister applauded for something she can't—or doesn't want to—do may create tension and cause unnecessary setbacks.

TWINS IN TRAINING
Allowing each toddler to reach his individual developmental milestones will help prevent potty training from becoming a competition between them.

Starting later

The likelihood is that the later you begin potty training, the easier it will be. Studies have shown, for example, that many children who start potty training before they are 18 months aren't completely trained until after the age of four; while those who don't start until after their second birthday are completely trained by the time they reach the age of three.

When is the best time to start potty training?

The best time to start encouraging your toddler in this new skill is when she is showing signs of readiness and has a settled and happy routine. Any disruptive event in your toddler's life could cause a setback in her behavior and make it a bad time to consider potty training.

Starting at the right time

You know your child best and can tell how much change or stress she can cope with. But if there are upheavals in her life, it makes sense to wait until her routine is back to normal, or at least more settled. Making even gentle demands on a child who's coping with disruption can cause distress and be unsuccessful.

Rain or shine?

Lots of moms start potty training when the weather is warm and their toddlers can run around lightly dressed—or, better still, not dressed at all. Your child will undoubtedly have a better chance of making it to the potty on time if she doesn't have to strip off layers of clothes first. But whatever

EASY DRESSING
If your toddler starts potty training in the summer, wearing less clothing will help her to master new skills.

the weather, if your toddler shows all the signs of being ready, that's the time to start teaching her—even if it's in the middle of winter. You can, after all, keep the house a little warmer so she can at least wear less when she's indoors.

When to wait

Put off potty training if your toddler is having to deal with any of the following situations:

★ starting daycare

★ starting with a new caregiver

★ a recent stay in the hospital (yours or hers)

★ moving to a new house

★ separation or divorce

★ the loss—by death or separation—of someone she was close to.

A new sibling

If you are expecting a new baby, the thought of having two in diapers may tempt you to think about potty training your toddler. But while she's getting used to sharing your attention with a new baby brother or sister, your toddler is probably going to be less cooperative than usual, at least for a while. Think about it from your point of view, too—do you want to be cleaning up puddles and dealing with potties while also caring for your newborn?

NEW ARRIVALS
Don't start potty training your toddler when the arrival of a new baby is imminent—give your child a chance to get used to her new sibling before you and she embark on this next step.

" Up until now, Jack hasn't paid much attention to anyone using the toilet, but **looking at pictures** of other toddlers on the potty has definitely helped **stimulate his interest.** "

JOANNA, mother of Jack, 26 months

Preparing your toddler

Before beginning potty training, you need to introduce your toddler to the potty. It's worth having one in the house from 18 months onward. You can also start teaching him the skills he'll need for using the potty. But remember—at this age, he's just getting familiar with the whole process and is not ready to be out of diapers.

First things first

Your toddler still has a long way to go before he's ready to start routinely using the potty. But the better prepared he is now, the easier it will be when he's ready to make the change.

First he needs to know what a potty is—and what it's used for. You may already have a potty—or perhaps you could take your toddler to the store to choose one. Having one in the house will give you the chance to explain all about it. Introducing the potty, however, needs to be done gradually and gently—too much pressure could discourage him. But there are lots of fun ways of getting him interested (see page 24).

Growing up

Encouraging your toddler's sense of independence will help lay down good foundations for successful potty training. He needs to be confident about trying things on his own—and, since most toddlers are eager to be in control, now is a good time to give him lots of opportunities to be "grown-up."

Paving the way

When it comes to potty training, your goal is to make the process as positive and natural for your toddler as possible. In this way, you'll stimulate his desire for independence, help him feel loved and valued, and boost your confidence as a parent, too.

One of the first steps toward this goal is to make sure your toddler is well prepared. As with every new skill, learning to use a potty is a step-by-step process, and your toddler needs lots of experience and opportunities to practice before he can really master it. Putting a potty in front of him and expecting him to use it when he has no concept

Potty or toilet?

Most toddlers learn how to use a potty before moving on to using the toilet. There are lots of reasons why a potty is best.

- It's portable—you can have it upstairs, downstairs, move it from room to room, and whisk it under your toddler's bottom just when he needs it! You can even take it with you on shopping trips or visits to friends or family.
- It's comfortable—generally, toddlers are happier to sit on a potty than on the toilet, which can be scary at first, even with a special seat on it.
- It's effective—your toddler's body is in more of a "squatting" position on a potty than on a toilet, making it easier to poop.

Potty hygiene

Putting a piece of toilet paper in the bottom before your toddler poops can make dirty potties easy to clean out. Dump the contents down the toilet before rinsing out. A regular wash with hot, soapy water will help prevent smells.

of going to the bathroom is at best likely to baffle him and at worst will create problems that may take many months to overcome.

Instead, you need to give him a chance to get used to the idea without any pressure to perform. For example, having a potty already in the bathroom, letting him see you and your partner use the toilet, introducing the language you plan to use, and making potty training as matter-of-fact as possible will help the change from diapers to potty progress more smoothly.

Choosing a potty

Potties come in specially molded plastic, making them light, easy to clean, and warm to sit on. When choosing a potty, bear in mind that it should be sturdy and durable,

PRACTICING WITH DOLLY
Sitting her dolly on a potty at the same time will make the introduction of potty training even more fun for your child.

Toilet seats

TOILET ACCESSORIES
If your child wants to use the toilet, a child seat and plastic stool will make the experience safe and comfortable.

Your toddler may want to imitate you and use the toilet instead of a potty. Rather than discouraging him, consider buying a special child toilet seat. For a toddler, sitting perched on the bowl of the toilet may be frightening as well as dangerous. Choose a seat that's comfortable and attaches firmly. You'll need a small, stable stool or plastic box next to the toilet, too, so your child can easily climb up to the seat. This will also help him stabilize himself with his feet while he's sitting there.

It's best to keep the seat permanently on the toilet so it's always ready when your toddler needs it. Other members of the family can simply remove it when they need to use the toilet themselves—encourage them to remember to replace it when they're finished.

---

with a broad, stable base so that it won't tip over when your toddler gets up. It should be curved inside for easy cleaning, with a molded back support and a slot for carrying.

A basic potty is inexpensive, but you can spend more for something more fun to help stimulate interest. You can choose from a wide variety, including potties molded into shapes such as animals and cars, or potties that play a tune when they are used.

Letting your toddler know that the potty is his is a great way of helping him feel in control. If he's interested, let him put stickers on it, or print his name on it with a permanent marker.

Useful features include:
● a splash guard—this is good for boys, who may have difficulty remembering to point their penis downward, although it's no guarantee that urine won't be accidentally sprayed over the edge. Girls can still use potties with a splash guard—they just need to be taught to sit with it at the back.
● a lid—this will keep any unpleasant odors trapped, which helps at other people's houses and when carrying and emptying the potty. If you are out in the car, a lid also means you can store a used potty in the trunk or on the floor of the car until you have a chance to empty it.

FUN FEATURES
Potties in bright colors or fun shapes will help to stimulate your toddler's interest in potty training.

How do I introduce the potty?

Introducing the potty to your toddler is the first step toward potty training. The best time to do this is at about 18 months. Having a potty in the house is all about getting your toddler used to seeing it around and giving you the chance to talk about what it's for. Remember that at this stage, your toddler is still not ready to start potty training.

Choose a spot

The best place for your toddler's potty is close to the family toilet. This will help her make the association between going to the bathroom and using the potty. If, however, she wants to move it around the house, then let her: feeling that the potty is under her control will help boost her sense of independence.

Toddlers love to imitate, so it helps if you feel relaxed about using the toilet when she's around. Going to the bathroom together will also help give you the chance to talk about what's happening and help her make the right connections.

Practice makes perfect

Whenever you can, encourage your toddler to sit on the potty. Initially, she may just want to explore it and play with it, but after a while she'll start to sit on it. At first she may do this only with her clothes on, but once she has practiced a few times, you can suggest she tries it with her diaper off.

If she enjoys sitting there, let her do so whenever she likes. The more familiar she is with her potty, the happier she'll be to use it when the time comes.

GETTING FAMILIAR
Allowing your child to play games with her new potty gets her familiar with it, as well as creating the opportunity to talk about what it's for.

Once your toddler has gotten used to the potty, try to make it part of your morning or evening routine. When she gets out of bed or before getting in the bathtub, you could suggest she sits on the potty for a little while.

Be patient

Initially, your toddler may show no interest in the potty or resist being asked to try sitting on it. If this is the case, don't push her. As the months go, by a little gentle encouragement may do no harm, but for now, it's best to leave her alone until she feels completely ready.

If she does pee or poop, show her that you're pleased, but don't get overexcited—too much praise might put her under pressure to perform again, and at this age she may choose to give up on the potty altogether rather than risk not getting your applause. It's early, and it was probably good timing rather than a sign to start potty training.

"LIKE A GROWNUP"
Give your child lots of praise when she does helpful things such as putting her toys away—this will boost her confidence and sense of independence.

Potty vocabulary

Potty training will be easier for your toddler if the same words are used by everyone in the house, and your toddler is already familiar with them. Which words you choose will depend on your personal preference, but they should be easy for your toddler to understand and use himself.

Bear in mind, however, that there will be times when your toddler, unaware of social niceties, may use these words in public! Most people are not offended by the words "poop" or "pee," and you will probably find that many other families use these or similar words.

Expert tips

• Sometimes even the most creative ideas to encourage your toddler to sit on his potty (see page 24) will fall flat if he's not ready. Rather than risk building resentment, ignore any mention of the potty until your toddler starts to show real interest himself.

• Never force your toddler to sit on the potty—getting angry or physically restraining him won't accomplish anything. In fact, it will have the opposite effect—your toddler will become fearful and may resist using the potty altogether for many months.

As your toddler gets older, you can teach him to say, "I need to go potty, please" as an acceptable alternative to a graphic description of what he needs to do.

Nurturing independence

Encouraging your toddler to be independent will help build his confidence and give him just the boost he needs to handle the change from diapers to potty. Toddlers are naturally eager to be in control and do things for themselves—even when they can't quite manage! But the more your toddler can do for himself, the happier he'll be.

● **Let him try** Your toddler loves showing you how smart he is, and your enthusiasm is always the best reward when he tries something new—even if he finds it difficult to master at first.

● **Give him lots of praise** This is especially important when he behaves in a "grown-up" way, whether it's putting his toys away or using his fork correctly.

● **Have realistic expectations** All children develop at different rates, so don't compare your toddler with others. Instead, watch him when he wants to do something for himself, be there for him if he needs your help, but let him feel as if he's done it on his own.

POTTIES ARE FUN
Let your toddler play with toys or look at books while he sits on his potty—or better still, read his favorite book to him.

Learning new skills

Helping your toddler learn how to use the potty isn't just about encouraging him to sit on one when he needs to pee or poop. He also needs to learn a few important practical skills.

● **Hand-washing** Teaching your toddler good cleaning habits now will serve him well when it comes to using the potty. Make hand washing part of his pre-meal routine—but encourage your toddler to do it for himself. Make sure he has easy access to a sink (a stable stool helps), and put the soap within reach. Liquid soap is less slippery for little fingers than bar soap. Make sure the water isn't too hot, and then leave him to it—the more control he has, the more grown-up he'll feel.

How can I get my toddler interested in the potty?

Although some toddlers are happy to be introduced to the potty at around 18 months, others remain blissfully uninterested for a lot longer. However, there are a number of fun tactics you could use to stimulate your toddler's interest. A little low-key motivation may be all that's needed to encourage her in the right direction.

Making it fun

You've done all the right things—there's a potty in the family bathroom, and you've told your toddler what it's for and encouraged her to try sitting on it. But she's still not interested. What can you do? It may be worth trying the following fun ideas:

★ looking together at a fun book about potties will help prepare your toddler

★ surrounding her potty with things to look at— her favorite books or toys

★ enlisting the help of an older sibling or friend— toddlers often idolize older children, and seeing them use the toilet may make the breakthrough

★ playing games together that involve her teddy bears or dolls using the potty

★ watching a video with her while she sits on the potty.

Your toddler needs to associate the potty with happy moments, so even if she sits on the potty then gets up seconds later without having done anything, give her lots of praise. Remember, at this stage, you are just introducing her to the idea of the potty.

PANTS AT THE READY
Buy some "big girl" underpants for your toddler. Show them to her and talk to her about what they're for. Tell her that one day, when she's ready, she'll be able to wear them.

• **Dressing and undressing** Your toddler will have much more success getting to the potty on time if he can handle the tricky business of pulling down his pants and underwear. Give him lots of opportunities to practice getting dressed and undressed himself, even if it sometimes seems simpler and quicker to take over and do it for him. Choosing stretchy, loose-fitting clothes without too many buttons or snaps will help him get dressed on his own.

HYGIENIC HABITS
Making hand-washing a part of your toddler's daily routine from an early age will ensure that she develops good hygiene habits to last her a lifetime.

Questions & Answers

My son is nearly two-and-a-half years old and has no interest in the potty at all. If I try to get him to sit on, it he just cries. What should I do?
Nothing. He's obviously not ready for potty training, and insisting that he sits on his potty is just upsetting him and making you frustrated. He's physically and emotionally unable to cope. Put the potty away, let him forget all about it, and try again in a month or so.

My two-year-old always wants me to do everything for him. He won't even try putting on his own shoes or doing a puzzle unless I'm there to help. How will he ever be potty-trained if he won't try anything for himself?
Some toddlers would rather not try to do anything at all than risk failure. He could be a natural perfectionist, or perhaps more has been expected of him than he can deliver. Make sure you're not setting unrealistic standards—this could damage his self-esteem and make him fearful of even trying. Instead, give him small things to do with you that you know he's capable of— helping to put the laundry in the washing machine or unpack the groceries—and praise him even when he just tries. Gradually, his confidence will start to grow. Meanwhile, keep potty training off the agenda until he's properly motivated.

" Martine was nearly two-and-a-half when she first **showed any interest** in her potty. Every time she asked to use it, I clapped and **sang her praises**. "

MONIQUE, mother of Martine, age three

3

First days out of diapers

Once your toddler is ready to begin potty training, stay calm and relaxed and things should proceed smoothly. Remember that the key point is to make using the potty seem as natural and normal as possible. With your praise—and maybe a few extra incentives—your toddler will enjoy taking this big step toward independence.

A gradual process

When you feel confident that your toddler is ready to begin potty training, you need to be ready to help and encourage her. With your active support, she is likely to reach dryness without much trouble—and will be happy and confident throughout the process.

For most toddlers, learning to use the potty successfully is a step-by-step process, and your toddler will progress through each stage at her own pace. Each child reaches dryness at a different age, so it's important not to talk about your toddler's achievements (or lack thereof) with other parents. Instead, be positive and remind yourself that she needs all your support and encouragement.

Ways to help

Your toddler may be grown-up enough to use a potty, but that doesn't mean she's ready to cope entirely on her own. For a while yet, you'll need to be on hand to remind her, help with her clothes, make sure she's wiped herself properly—and even offer some small incentives when the novelty of potty training begins to wane. Giving her as much attention as possible during this phase will help her work toward success.

Trial and error

You've introduced your toddler to the potty, and she enjoys sitting on it and has even had a few successes with it. She understands what it's for and is by now showing most—or maybe all—of the signs that say she's ready for potty training (see pages 8–9).

Remember that, to a large extent, learning to use the potty is trial and error—although some toddlers go from diapers to underpants with few accidents, for others it's a slower, more gradual change.

Checklist

Once you've decided that your toddler is ready for potty training, make sure you are, too. You will need:

• lots of pairs of underpants—there are bound to be accidents, so you need plenty of spares

• time at home—try to start potty training during a quiet time so your toddler isn't distracted or coping with change

• a plan of action—are you going to ditch diapers from day one, or start off with training pants (see page 29)? Think about how you are going to handle accidents—deciding now will help you be consistent

• a stash of rewards and/or incentives (see Ways to motivate, pages 34–35)—having her favorite books or videos nearby will help you when a little gentle persuasion is needed.

GOOD-BYE TO DIAPERS
Putting on "big boy's pants" for the first time is an exciting step toward independence for your toddler.

The important point is to make the whole process as relaxed and natural as possible.

There are different ways to go about potty training—some parents like to start their toddlers off in training pants (see box opposite); others opt to go straight into underpants. If you can't decide which method is best for your toddler, talk to your healthcare provider. Whichever way you choose, following these suggested steps will help the first few days of potty training run smoothly.

Step one
A few days before you start potty training.

• Increase the opportunities your toddler has for sitting on the potty, especially at those key moments, such as after a meal, when she's more likely to poop or pee. Never force her to stay there longer than she wants to—even just a few seconds is fine.

• After the first couple of mornings or afternoons, let her run around and play for extended sessions without her diaper on. Keep a close eye on her—you might be able to tell in advance if something is about to happen!

• If she does pee or poop without reaching the potty, be matter-of-fact. Tell her to let you know when she's wet because then you can change her quickly so she's comfortable and dry again. Being aware that she's peed or pooped is her first important step toward recognizing it before it happens.

Step two

On the day you decide to start.

• Put the diapers away and get out her new "big girl pants" or training pants (see box below). Explain to your toddler that today she doesn't need her diaper. If she can put the pants on herself, all the better—

REWARDING SUCCESS
Keep a supply of favorite treats handy to reward your child's successes.

Expert tips

Do dress your toddler in clothes she can easily manage herself. Pull-up pants with elastic waistbands, skirts, and dresses are best, while zippers, snaps, or clasps are difficult for small fingers.

Do tell everyone who cares for your toddler that you are potty training so that they can help, too.

Don't give up too quickly—even if you have just a few successes, it's worth persevering. Switching back to diapers occasionally because it's more convenient may confuse your toddler.

Don't expect too much—your toddler is still getting used to "holding it," so don't forget to take the potty with you on car trips or shopping trips (see pages 48–51).

Disposable training pants

Disposable training pants can be pulled up and down like underpants but have the extra padding of diapers and side seams that can be torn so they can be quickly removed. Some parents use them as an intermediate step, but others take the plunge and do away with diapers completely.

Advantages

• Your toddler can put them on and take them off just like real underpants.
• They absorb any accidents without soiling her clothes.

Disadvantages

• Your toddler won't know when she's wet—making the link between peeing and needing the potty much harder.
• She may treat them just like diapers and give up trying to reach the potty altogether.

I've just started potty training my toddler. When can I expect her to be dry?

Starting potty training is an exciting moment for most parents, since it brings with it the inviting prospect of life without diapers. It's also a big step forward for your child in terms of her independence. But don't rush it—the process of becoming totally dry can take some time, and each child will achieve dryness at a different age, so try not to have predetermined expectations.

How it happens

Some children get the hang of using the potty within a few days—these are usually the older ones. Many more—and especially toddlers who find change difficult to handle—take several months. This is because learning to use the potty is a step-by-step process, and children need lots of experience and practice in different situations before they can really master it. Here are the different stages your toddler needs to go through.

Stage one

Recognizing when she's peed or pooped. You can help by getting her to sit on the potty or toilet at key moments, such as first thing in the morning when she wakes up, or after a meal.

GOOD TIMING
Encouraging your toddler to sit on her potty or the toilet first thing in the morning when she probably needs to pee will help her to recognize when she has urinated.

Stage two

Telling you she needs to go—there won't be much time between words and actions in the early days.

Stage three

Being able to "hold it." Having enough control to wait while you find the potty or a toilet can take a few more months, since the strengthening of the bowel and bladder muscles happens gradually.

Clean and dry

Your toddler will probably discover how to stay clean—using her potty rather than her diaper for a poop—around the same time she starts to stay dry. This is because urination usually occurs with the bowel movements, so it is difficult for your toddler to differentiate between the two acts.

HANGING ON
In time, your toddler will gain the control needed to hold it while you find a toilet or potty.

TELLING YOU WHAT SHE NEEDS
Being able to tell you that she needs to pee or poop is a major step forward in the process of potty-training your toddler. Keep a potty nearby at first, since you may not get much warning.

EASY ON, EASY OFF
Dress your toddler in clothes he can easily manage. This will help him master the skills required to use the potty.

your toddler will love being so independent and grown-up.

- Remind her to ask you for her potty when she feels that she needs it—try to have it close by so she can reach it easily and quickly (one potty upstairs and one downstairs is a good idea).
- Watch the clock—if she hasn't gone for while, if she had a large cup of juice an hour or so ago, or if it's around the time she usually poops, give her a few timely reminders.
- Encourage your toddler with lots of praise and remind her how grown-up she is.
- When she has an accident, don't react negatively—just remind your toddler what the potty is for and change her without a fuss.

Working toward dryness

Don't expect too much from your toddler during these first few days out of diapers. Can you remember how she learned to walk? It's unlikely that she just stood up and walked across the room one day. Instead, she would have tottered and stumbled for many days before getting the hang of it.

As with walking, potty training is usually a gradual process. While there are toddlers—especially the older ones—who are dry from day one with hardly an accident, there are many more who take their time learning how to stay dry and clean. Here's what will and what won't help along the way.

"John learned to use the potty quite quickly, but he still needs a little help now and then. He finds elasticated waistbands easiest to cope with on his own."

MIRIAM, mother of John, now three

What works

• Taking it slowly—getting to grips with the different stages of toilet training (see pages 30-31) can take a while, and your toddler will move on when she's ready.

• Lots of praise—tell your toddler that you are proud of what she's done when she tries to use her potty (even if she doesn't always manage it successfully). But don't get too excited—too much praise may make your toddler nervous and worried about failing next time and discourage her from trying.

• Staying nearby—your toddler may be ready to use the potty, but she's not yet grown-up enough to cope alone.

• Expecting accidents—it's inevitable that there will be some, so don't be surprised or impatient when they happen (see page 37).

• Staying calm—when accidents do happen, simply clean up without commenting and remind your toddler to try using her potty next time.

What doesn't work

• Forcing your toddler to stay on the potty—this will only scare her and make her much less likely to cooperate.

• Talking to others about her progress—or lack of it—in front

Daytime naps

Switching back into diapers for daytime naps may help your toddler avoid accidents, but it does send mixed messages that could confuse her. Instead, you could:

• encourage her to use her potty before putting her down for a nap

• put a plastic cover under the sheet of her crib to protect the mattress in case she does have an accident

• if she falls asleep unexpectedly, protect the car seat, sofa, or stroller with a folded towel.

DIAPERLESS NAPS
Avoid using diapers just for daytime naps, since this could confuse your toddler. Instead, take precautions to minimize the mess if accidents happen.

of her. Any sense of disappointment or impatience on your part will be picked up by your toddler.

• Putting on pressure—your toddler will progress at her own speed, and pushing her faster than she can cope with may make her nervous and unable to poop at all.

• Punishing your toddler—if she's not interested in using the potty or has an accident, getting angry will only make matters worse.

• Showing signs of disgust—dealing with dirty potties or cleaning up a

poopy accident can be unpleasant, but disdainful comments or gestures will upset your toddler.

Just for girls

Most toddlers are happy for their parents to wipe their bottoms for them, and most parents are happy to do it, since getting it right can take a lot of practice. If, however, your toddler is eager to do it herself, it's important to teach her how to do it correctly. Explain to her that she must move the toilet paper from the

Expert tips

Don't expect your toddler to use her potty on command. In the early days, she'll pee only when she feels the need. She'll be at least three years old before you can remind her to go to the bathroom prior to leaving the house.

Do be careful about the words you use. Avoid telling her she's a "good" girl for using the potty or a "naughty girl" for having an accident, since this makes using the potty a moral issue.

her front toward her bottom, especially if she has pooped. This is to prevent bacteria from passing from her bowel to her vagina or urethra, where it could cause infection.

For now, she may be happy for you to keep wiping her bottom for her. If not, see if she will let you have the "last wipe" or a quick look to check that the job has been done properly. When she's just peed, a dab with the toilet paper should be sufficient to keep her dry.

"GUESS WHAT I CAN DO"
Letting your toddler call Grandma with news of his achievements will help keep him interested in his new goals.

Just for boys

Most toddlers poop and pee at the same time, so it makes sense to teach your son to sit on the potty when he's first getting the hang of potty training. Once he's happy using his potty, he may want to try standing up to pee (see page 41 for teaching tips), but even when he's graduated to the toilet, if he wants to continue sitting, he should be allowed to do so.

When it comes to bottom-wiping, your son will probably be happy for you to do this for him. If not, see if you can persuade him to let you have the "last wipe" or just check to see that the job has been done properly.

Ways to motivate

It's common for toddlers to start to lose interest in potty training. For some, lots of praise, along with reminders about how grown-up they are, is enough to keep them going. Toddlers also love feeling in control, so gradually giving her more responsibility, such as preparing the toilet paper or helping you empty the potty into the toilet and flush it, may help keep her interested.

For others, more tangible rewards work best—as long as you avoid letting your toddler dictate the prize! It's likely that, once your toddler is on the way to being permanently dry,

she won't need these extra incentives. Keep the rewards small:

- make her a sticker chart—each time she uses her potty, she can choose a sticker and put it on her chart
- let her have one of her favorite treats or a cup of her favorite juice each time she has a success
- calling a grandparent or other relative to tell them about her triumphs will help her feel grown-up
- show her how "magic water" works—drip some blue food coloring into the toilet, and your toddler will be thrilled to see the water turn green when she pees
- put several favorite books next to the toilet so she can read them when she has to go.

STAR PERFORMANCE
Make a chart together so your toddler can stick on a star each time she uses her potty. This will help keep her motivated.

Questions & Answers

My daughter drinks a lot during the day, and I'm worried that this will make potty training harder. Should I restrict the amount of fluid she drinks?
Cutting down on the number of drinks your toddler has during the day may help her avoid accidents, but it's not good for her health. If your daughter is thirsty, she needs to drink. And in fact, needing to use the potty frequently is

more likely to help her get the hang of potty training, since she'll have more chances to practice.

My toddler's due to start nursery school in a few months, but she's not potty-trained yet. What should I do?
Nursery schools often insist that children are out of diapers before they start. But this isn't always the case—a daycare center that takes children from a few

months old will often help with potty training. If you are planning to send your child to nursery school, ask them about their policy. If they would like your toddler to be dry before she starts, you'll need to plan ahead and decide when to start introducing the potty. Bear in mind, however, that if your toddler simply is not ready, starting her too soon may actually slow the process.

" I quickly came to realize that **accidents** are an integral part of potty training! Whenever Lucy has one I give **her a hug** and reassure her that she'll get it right the next time. **"**

DAVID, father of Lucy, nearly three

What to expect

Some toddlers sail through potty training with few hitches. Others seem to take two steps forward and one back. Knowing what to expect during potty training—from accidents to toilet fears—will help you support your toddler along the way, boosting his confidence and making the whole process seem entirely normal and natural.

All about accidents

Learning how to stay dry is a big step for your toddler—and understanding what's likely to happen along the way will help you tune in to his needs and respond in the best and most effective way possible.

Life is so exciting for your toddler, it's sometimes easy for him to forget about using the potty. Accidents are entirely natural—especially when you first start—and they can happen for lots of reasons. Coping with accidents can be frustrating, but dealing with them calmly will help prevent them from becoming an issue for you or your toddler.

How to react

Your toddler is bound to have accidents while he's learning to stay dry—and even once he's consistently using the potty, there will be times when he'll wet himself. How you react, however, will have a big impact on your toddler.

Of course, if your toddler is all dressed up, ready to go to a party and suddenly a river starts flowing down his legs, keeping your cool may be a bigger challenge than when an accident happens just before bathtime. But the more calm and relaxed you can be, the less threatened your toddler will feel by his mistakes—and the more confidence he will then have that next time, he'll be able to get it right.

Dos and don'ts when accidents happen

• **Do** commiserate—wet underpants are uncomfortable and even embarrassing for your toddler.
• **Do** be matter-of-fact—simply say, "Let's get some dry underpants, and next time you can try to remember to use your potty."

Expert tip

Most children achieve daytime dryness and cleanliness before they can go through the night without a diaper. Many also continue to wear diapers for daytime naps. Staying dry and clean at night can often be more of a challenge, so don't expect your toddler to clear this hurdle too soon (see pages 52–59).

• **Do** clean up without comment—keep a bucket and cloth handy.
• **Do** keep trying—sometimes it may feel that potty training is going on forever, and lots of parents wonder if they'll ever see an end to diapers. But all toddlers get there in the end, and staying positive throughout will help give your toddler the confidence he needs to succeed.
• **Don't** make a fuss—remember that accidents are as inevitable as falling down while learning to walk.

My toddler can use the potty but she still wets herself. Why is this?

Almost all toddlers will have several accidents before they become completely dry during the day—after all, their muscles have only just developed enough to allow them to have any control at all over their bowel and bladder, and it will be quite a while yet before they are able to hold it indefinitely.

Possible causes of accidents

If your toddler has very frequent accidents, it may be that she just isn't ready to use the potty yet, in which case it's best to go back to diapers for a few more weeks before trying again. Often, though, accidents happen for other, more mundane reasons, and dealing with these can help you put potty training back on the fast track.

★ **Tiredness** When your toddler is in need of a nap, she'll be less aware that she needs the potty— and also less able to hold it. Make sure that she doesn't miss her naps.

★ **Slowness** Some toddlers wait until the last minute before looking for the potty—again, occasional reminders from you will help.

COPING WITH ACCIDENTS
There are many reasons why accidents happen. Clearing up quickly and calmly, and offering reassurance when they do occur, will help keep your child's potty training on track.

★ **Nervousness or excitement** If your toddler is overwhelmed by something or coping with a new situation, she may lose control of her bladder. Birthday parties or weekend trips are common occasions for accidents to happen.

★ **Concentration** When your toddler is deeply absorbed in an activity, she'll be more prone to accidents—stay nearby so you can remind her to use the potty if necessary.

★ **Lack of coordination** Struggling with pants or tights can result in last-minute accidents. Always be on hand in case help is needed, and make sure your toddler is wearing clothes that are easy to remove.

★ **Pressure** Independent-minded toddlers may choose not to use the potty if you push too hard and make too big an issue of it.

★ **Stress** Any big change in your toddler's life— such as the arrival of a baby brother or sister, moving, getting a new caregiver, or starting daycare—may cause a temporary setback in using the potty.

IN NEED OF A NAP
Accidents are sometimes more common when your child is tired and in need of sleep—keep an eye on the clock and make sure she doesn't miss her daytime naps.

Bowel accidents

These can happen for all the same reasons as wetting accidents. Sometimes loose stools or constipation can also make it hard for a toddler to control herself.

★ **Loose stools** Your toddler will be less aware that she needs the potty if her stools are soft, which can happen if she's sick, or if she's eating more fiber or drinking more fruit juice than usual.

★ **Constipation** If your toddler is constipated (see page 43), bowel movements can be painful. This may encourage her to hang on as long as possible, until she just can't wait anymore and the movement comes when she least expects it.

BUSY DAYS
*There may be times
when your toddler
is so engrossed in
what she's doing
that she'll forget
to go to the
bathroom.*

● Don't punish your toddler—
getting angry, demanding an apology,
or looking for a confession will scare
him and delay his progress.
● Don't leave him in wet pants—
trying to teach him a lesson by
not changing him will upset and
humiliate him.
● Don't tell him he's a baby—
this won't encourage grown-up
behavior.

"I'm a big boy now"

Once your toddler is happy on
the potty, he may want to start
using the toilet. Making the toilet a
comfortable and safe place to be
will help with the transition.
Some children, however,
develop fears about using
the toilet (see page 42). Helping
your toddler overcome any worries
he has may take time and patience,
but your loving support and
understanding will help motivate
him to try to use the toilet.

Getting used to the toilet is
especially useful when you are away
from home (see pages 46–51),
and it is necessary if your toddler is
going to be starting nursery school
soon. He will feel a lot safer if you
put a child-sized toilet seat on the
regular seat for him to sit on—and
he'll need a sturdy stool or box so
he can climb up and down by

*" Charlotte has been dry for months, but she
still has the odd accident. When I ask her
what happened, she says, 'I forgot!' I think
she sometimes just gets so absorbed in what
she's doing, she does genuinely 'forget'. "*

DENISE, mother of Charlotte, three years three months

Expert tip

If your toddler has an accident on the carpet or furniture, it's best to deal with it as quickly as possible. After getting your child into dry, clean pants, flush any poop down the toilet, then sponge carpets or sofas with cold water. Working from the center out will help avoid a water stain. If necessary, use some carpet or upholstery shampoo.

himself (see page 19). This will also provide a surface for him to put his feet on when he's sitting on the toilet. Make sure he can reach the toilet paper and encourage him to stand on the stool when he's finished so he can wash his hands at the sink, too.

Tips for boys

To start with, your son may be happier sitting on the toilet to pee—many boys take a while to get used to standing up. At some point, however, he'll want to be like his daddy or the other boys at daycare. Help him along by:

• making sure the toilet seat will stay in a raised position—if it falls your child will be scared and possibly injured

• teaching him to raise the toilet seat when he needs to pee and to put it down afterward

QUICK CHANGE
When accidents happen, change your toddler into dry clothes quickly and calmly.

Urinary tract infections

Sometimes children have repeated accidents because of a medical problem such as a urinary tract infection. These are more common in girls than boys and make bladder control very difficult. If your toddler is eager to use the potty but seems unable to "hold it," or has been dry for a while and then starts having accidents again, this may be the cause. Often, there are no symptoms, although sometimes your toddler may have:

• a fever

• pain when urinating

• blood in the urine.

Urinary tract infections need medical attention, so you should take your child to see your healthcare provider as soon as possible if you are at all concerned.

TEMPTING HIM ONTO THE TOILET
If your child seems concerned about using the toilet, offer lots of encouragement until he feels ready to give it a try.

Expert tip

Always keep a good supply of dry underpants within easy reach. Bear in mind, however, that if your toddler has an accident, his outerwear will probably be wet, too, so you'll also need to keep some dry pants ready for a quick change.

- offering target practice—put some toilet-paper "boats" in the toilet and get him to try to "sink" them: this will help him perfect his aim
- keeping a cloth and cleaner handy—while he's practicing, be prepared for unexpected splashes.

Toilet fears

- "I don't like the toilet"
Some children take a lot longer than others to feel comfortable using the toilet (long after they are dry and clean) and will use one only if there is absolutely no other choice—for example, at someone else's house. It won't do any harm for your toddler to keep using the potty for now—and in time, he'll realize that everyone else uses the toilet safely and happily, so there's no reason why he shouldn't, too. Meanwhile, offer him lots of encouragement, let him see you and your partner using the toilet, and, when he wants to try, make

sure you are nearby with words
of reassurance.

● "I don't want to stand up"
If your son isn't interested in
standing at the toilet, don't worry—
let him sit down until he feels ready
to try standing. There's no hurry,
and putting him under pressure
will only make him feel anxious.

● "I'm scared of the noise"
Fear of flushing may stop your
toddler from using the toilet. Don't
force him to watch or listen to the
flush—this may make his fear even
worse. Instead, let him leave the
bathroom first. Then build up his
confidence gradually—start by
flushing the toilet when he's in
earshot but not in the room; then
encourage him to stand in the
doorway while you flush; finally,
hold his hand or give him a

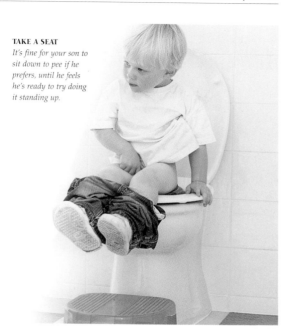

TAKE A SEAT
*It's fine for your son to
sit down to pee if he
prefers, until he feels
he's ready to try doing
it standing up.*

Constipation and how to deal with it

Constipation can develop for
a number of different reasons,
including:

● too much pressure to perform
during potty training

● fear of using the toilet—especially
when away from home.

What happens
The longer your toddler fails to
poop, the harder and drier it
becomes. Having a bowel movement
is then difficult and painful—which
can discourage him from going again.

What to do
Usually, diet and lifestyle changes can
solve the problem. Make sure your
toddler is getting plenty of fiber in his
diet—especially fresh and dried fruit
(raisins, prunes, and apricots). Make
sure he's drinking lots of fluids—
especially fruit juice—and take him
outside every day for fresh air and
exercise. A little Vaseline applied to
his anus may also help ease the
movement. Never give your child
laxatives unless your healthcare
provider recommends them.

When to see the doctor
If your toddler doesn't have a bowel
movement for four or five days; if
he has abdominal pain or vomiting;
or if the above methods don't work,
your toddler may need medical help.

Progress seems to be slow. Will my daughter ever be out of diapers?

If your toddler is taking potty training slowly, you may wonder whether she'll ever be out of diapers. You may even start to feel anxious or irritated by her lack of progress, especially if you see other children catching on earlier and faster. As with all skills, however, children go at their own pace—and they all get there in the end, even when it comes to potty training.

Staying positive

Don't let your feelings about your toddler's progress—or lack of it—affect your relationship with her. You can't force her to use the potty - after all, only she can control her bladder and her bowel. Instead:

★ remember that potty training isn't a race— comparing your toddler with others is unfair

★ accept that accidents are normal—even toddlers who've used the potty successfully for months make mistakes now and again

★ don't let it dent your confidence—your daughter's potty training is no reflection on your ability as a parent

★ ignore other people's comments—if necessary, explain that your daughter is going at her own pace and you have every confidence in her

★ hide your true feelings—even when it's hard not to feel concerned or unhappy, don't show your toddler. Not only will it be dispiriting for her, she may start to depend on your negative feelings as a good way to get more attention.

INDIVIDUAL PROGRESS
Your child will get the hang of potty training when she's ready and no sooner. If her friends seem to catch on quicker, be patient and stay positive—she'll get there in the end.

hug while you flush. Slowly but surely, with your patience and encouragement, he'll realize there is nothing to fear.

● "I want my diaper"

Lots of toddlers are happy to use the potty or toilet for peeing but insist on having their diaper on for poops, perhaps because it gives them a feeling of security. The best way to approach this is to do as your toddler asks but, at the same time, let him know that when he's ready, he'll be able to manage using the potty or toilet instead. As long as you don't create any pressure, it's likely that your toddler will put aside diapers for good in his own time.

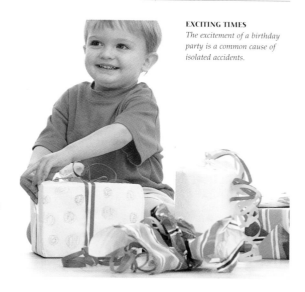

EXCITING TIMES
The excitement of a birthday party is a common cause of isolated accidents.

Questions & Answers

My daughter is two years and two months old and has been dry in the daytime for quite a few weeks, but she's still not able to control her bowel movement. She knows when she's done a poop in her pants—and comes and tells me. I thought children became clean before they became dry?

Your daughter is doing very well if she is already dry, since she's still quite young. Try not to worry—in time, she'll become clean, too. Meanwhile, give her lots of praise for all her successes and remind her that she can also use a potty for pooping. You can give her a helping

hand by keeping an eye on her routine—if she normally needs to poop after lunch or when she wakes up in the morning, watch for the signs and make sure her potty is close by.

At first, I tried not to get annoyed when Cody wet himself, but now I'm beginning to lose my patience. I get so irritated, especially since he knows how to use the potty. Sometimes I just want to yell at him. What should I do?

Potty training demands lots of patience, and sometimes it's hard to be sympathetic, especially if you feel your toddler should

know better by now. Maybe you think he's being stubborn, or getting at you on purpose. Or you might be worried that he's taking a long time to get dry—especially compared with your friends' toddlers. Trying to cover up negative feelings can sometimes create extra pressure. Instead, rather than showing your toddler how you feel by yelling at him, tell him how you feel: "Mommy's crabby today because she's had to do lots of wiping up." Your toddler needs to know that wet or dirty pants aren't a good thing—but he shouldn't be made to feel that he's a bad boy himself.

" I took a potty **everywhere** with me until my daughter was three. Most people who saw her using it in a parking lot or on a side street just **smiled** or looked the other way! "

JACKIE, mother of Jocelyn, age three

5

Out and about

Most toddlers have accidents while being potty-trained—which may make the prospect of going out pretty daunting. But worries about mishaps shouldn't stop you from taking your toddler shopping, visiting friends, or going on vacation. As long as you plan ahead, visits—long or short—can still be fun and hassle-free.

Planning ahead

Unless your toddler masters the art of using a potty in a couple of days, at some point in the early stages of potty training you'll have to leave the house, which means closing the front door on your nearest potty and toilet. There may be occasions in the very early days—such as a long car trip—when you feel it's best to put your toddler back in diapers, but a little preparation should make everyday outings go smoothly.

It's best to set out expecting an accident instead of crossing your fingers and hoping it won't happen. Without a travel potty at hand, or at least a change of clothes and some idea of where the nearest public restroom is, you may find you need to turn around and head home because of wet pants before you've even reached your destination.

Taking a potty out with you is useful with young toddlers, but as they get older, you may find they prefer not to do something private in public places. Getting your child familiar with different types of toilets as early as possible will help when you are out and about. And for those times when there's only a nearby tree or bush to hide behind, feeling comfortable about peeing outdoors can save the day.

Traveling long distances

Until your toddler is 100 percent reliable, traveling could make vacations more challenging.

- Airports and airplanes have toilets—if necessary, ask to cut in line rather than put your toddler at risk of having an accident.
- On long car trips, plan breaks so your toddler can use a toilet at regular intervals.
- Avoid giving her carbonated drinks; these may stimulate her bladder and make her pee more frequently.

Travel potties

One of the best options when you are stepping out the front door with your potty-training toddler in tow is to take a travel potty with you. Different types available include:

- those that fold flat, yet can be opened in seconds—they are used with absorbent liners that are leak-proof and airtight to prevent spills and smells

- a simple lidded version—ideal for older children who have graduated to using the toilet; you can also invest in a portable toilet seat that's useful for vacations.

I'm worried about going shopping. What do I do if my son needs a toilet?

It's a good idea to stay close to home for the first few stages of potty training, but for practical as well as social reasons, there will come a time when you need to take your toddler out. Leaving the safety of your home can be intimidating, but as long as you're prepared, there are lots of ways you can help your son when he needs the toilet.

Tips for trouble-free outings

Taking your toddler out while potty training means planning ahead—and not being embarrassed when nature calls!

★ Take a potty with you—you can use it in the car, at the park, or down a quiet side street.

★ Pack a spare change of clothes—remember that your toddler's outerwear will probably also be wet, so take spare pants or a skirt as well as underpants.

★ Keep a pack of baby wipes handy just in case you're faced with a major cleanup.

★ Protect the car and/or stroller seat with a folded towel or plastic bag.

★ Encourage your toddler to use the potty just before you go out, but if he doesn't want to, or he tries but nothing happens, leave it at that.

BEFORE YOU GO OUT
Note when your toddler last used his potty before going shopping, and encourage him to sit on it again just before you go out. This way, you'll have a sense of when he might need it again.

★ Make a mental note of where the nearest public restroom is, so if he needs to go, you'll know exactly where to head.

★ Note when he last used his potty so you have a sense of when he'll need to use it again.

If nature calls

★ React as quickly as possible, however inconvenient the situation.

★ If you don't have a potty with you or you are some distance from a public restroom, go to the nearest fast-food restaurant—you can usually take your child to the bathroom even if you're not a customer.

★ Don't be embarrassed about cutting in line— if you explain briefly that your toddler can't hold it, most people will smile and let you skip to the front.

★ If you are in a store, ask for directions to the nearest restroom, or, if you have a potty with you, take your toddler to the back of the store to use it.

★ In a building without a public restroom, ask if you can use the staff facilities.

★ If you are out in the park, nip behind a tree with your toddler.

★ If your toddler wets his pants—or worse— stay calm. Take him somewhere private so you can clean him up and change him.

PLAN AHEAD
When you take your toddler out shopping, make sure you know where the nearest public restroom is so you can get there quickly if the need arises.

Expert tip

Try not to be tempted to switch back into diapers for convenience's sake when you are out and about, since this will give your toddler mixed messages. Consistency is important—and if you are serious about potty training, you should try not to confuse your child by using diapers when it's not really necessary.

BE PREPARED
Make sure you have everything you need—spare clothes, wipes, tissues—close at hand when you go out with your diaperless toddler.

• Cups of juice may help keep your child quiet on a long trip, but bear in mind that drinking lots of fluid while you are traveling will also make her need to use the toilet more frequently.

• Keep toilet paper and toilet wipes handy—in your bag or in a pocket in the car rather than at the bottom of a suitcase.

Away from home

Some toddlers find unfamiliar places unsettling and may even regress in their potty training. This might be because they feel disoriented, or the toilet isn't like the one at home. Overcome any setbacks by:

• taking a potty with you—don't use a vacation as a chance to get her used to using a toilet instead

• if she has already progressed to the toilet, take your child's toilet seat with you

❝I encouraged Jenna to use the toilet from early on, and she loved feeling grown-up. This has made outings much easier, since she's happy to use a public toilet—checking them out in restaurants or department stores has become one of her favorite pastimes!❞

SALLY, mother of Jenna, three-and-a-half

• accept that she may want you to stay with her when she uses the toilet.

Peeing outdoors

There will be times when there's not a toilet in sight and your child has no choice but to pee outdoors—whether you're enjoying a family picnic and there are only trees nearby or you're traveling in the car and the side of a quiet road will have to do.

With boys, it helps if they are already used to peeing standing up—watching daddy can help encourage your son to learn this skill (see also page 41).

HANDY EXTRAS
Travel potties with absorbent liners can be useful when you are between destinations.

For girls, it's a little more tricky—you can help by supporting your daughter in a squatting position. Or, if she's eager to manage on her own, make sure she takes off her underpants first, since holding her clothing out of the way will be hard.

ON THE ROAD
If your child needs a toilet when she's in the car, stop as soon as you can.

Questions & Answers

My husband is taking our three-year-old daughter on a long car trip to visit his parents, and he's worried about using the restrooms at highway service stations. Will he have to take her into the men's bathroom?
At this age, children should always be accompanied when they use a public restroom. But while it's acceptable for both boys and girls to go into the women's bathroom with their mother or female caregiver, and for little boys to go with their father into the men's room, dads can find it hard when they're with their daughters. Unless the men's room is a single, lockable bathroom that

admits only one man at a time, it would not be appropriate for your daughter to use it. Fortunately, many restaurant chains and service stations now have "parent and child" or "special needs" facilities, which both men and women can use. Your automobile association may be able to tell you where suitable facilities are located along your route.

When we're out shopping, my five-year-old will hold it until we get home rather than use a strange toilet. How can I help him feel comfortable with using a toilet other than his own?
It's very common for young children to feel uncomfortable in a strange bathroom, and

as they get older, they may worry about lack of privacy or getting locked in. Public restrooms (including school bathrooms) can also be smelly and unpleasant. But "holding it" for long periods can cause constipation as well as being very uncomfortable. Get your son used to a range of toilets by visiting different bathrooms together—at a friend's house, at the mall, or at the library, for example. Initially, he doesn't need to use the toilet—just let him look. Then, if he's happy to use the toilet, stay with him. Gradually, he'll get used to different kinds of bathrooms, types of flushes, and types of door locks and become confident using toilets other than his own.

" Although Faye is dry during the day, her nighttime diapers are still wet at least every other morning. I'll **wait a little longer** and then try her without one for the **whole night.** "

HELENA, mother of Faye, nearly three

Dry at night

Your clever toddler is now dry during the day—and both of you are enjoying the freedom of life without diapers. For a while, as his bladder continues maturing, he'll still need diapers at night. But watch for the signs, and at some point before his fourth birthday, he'll be ready to go diaperless at night, too.

Next step forward

For your toddler, staying dry while asleep demands more control than staying dry when awake. Some children still need diapers for daytime naps even if they are otherwise dry. As time goes on, however, and his bladder grows and strengthens, your child will reach the stage where he can go the whole night without needing to pee—or at least wake up and use the toilet or the potty when he feels the urge.

Some toddlers decide diapers are babyish and decide on their own to give them up. With others, it's simply a question of watching for the signs that your child is capable of managing without them. Most children are dry at night by the time they are four.

It is likely that, as with daytime dryness, there will be accidents along the way. Preparing the bed with a waterproof mattress pad and keeping a supply of dry nightwear and sheets will help you and your child get back to sleep quickly. If accidents are still happening when your child starts school, don't worry—there's lots you can do to help him become dry.

Is he ready?

Just because he's dry during the day, your child won't automatically become dry at night. Although your toddler can "hold it" during the day before needing to use his potty, controlling his bladder during the night is a different matter altogether. This is because he sleeps for a long time—holding it for 10–12 hours requires a strong bladder—and is unable to respond to the bladder's signal that it is full. Until his bladder matures further, he will continue to pee during the night, blissfully unaware of what's happening. It's unlikely that your child's bladder will reach the required level of maturity for a while yet.

Expert tip

Several diaper manufacturers make diapers especially for larger toddlers or young children who may have grown out of standard-sized diapers but still need reliable protection during the night.

But how do you know when he is ready to leave off his nighttime diapers? Some toddlers, usually the older ones, decide for themselves—although this doesn't necessarily mean they can last until morning without needing to pee.

Avoid ditching the diapers too soon by waiting until you see the following signs:
- he regularly wakes up with a dry diaper
- he can go three or four hours during the day without peeing
- occasionally he wakes up during the night because he needs to pee.

My son is out of daytime diapers now. When will he be dry at night?

Once your toddler is happily out of diapers during the day, the next big step is becoming dry at night. This may seem like an impossible goal right now, but when he's developmentally ready, your son will be able to hold it until morning, and give up nighttime diapers, too.

What to expect

Although a few toddlers automatically become dry at night once they've mastered daytime control, most still wear a diaper at night for some time afterward. If your toddler is still peeing every couple of hours during the day and always wakes up in the morning with a wet diaper, it's likely he'll wet the bed if you take a chance and try putting him to bed without a diaper.

Moving toward dryness

Since you can't teach your son to hold it until morning—this can only happen with greater maturity of his bladder—there's little you can do to hurry things along. Instead, watch for the signs that he is moving toward dryness (see page 53) and avoid putting on any pressure, which may make him anxious. He will probably be dry all night by the time he is four, but it's worth bearing in mind that many five-year-olds are still not 100 percent dry.

SWEET DREAMS
Don't make an issue out of your toddler's becoming dry at night, since this could make him anxious—nighttime dryness will happen as soon as his bladder is mature enough.

Nights without diapers

Once your child is ready to go without nighttime diapers, there are ways you can help him become dry at night:

● make sure he feels good about sleeping without a diaper—as with daytime training, he needs to be ready emotionally as well as physically

● explain to your child that there is a waterproof cover on the bed so that it doesn't matter if he accidentally pees in the night

● put a potty nearby in case he wakes up before morning needing to pee

● put a night-light in his room so he can see what he's doing if he does wake up and needs the potty

● let him know that he can call you if he wants to—being awake at night can be frightening for small children, and your toddler is more likely to

TAKING PRECAUTIONS
Talk to your child about not wearing a diaper at night, and show him that you're putting a special cover on his mattress so that, if an accident should occur, it doesn't matter.

Expert tip

Wetting accidents will soak right through your child's mattress, making it hard to dry—and harder still to remove the smell. Instead, before he goes diaperless for the night, protect your child's bed with a full-size waterproof sheet or mattress cover under the fitted sheet, and tell him what it's there for.

NIGHTTIME ACCIDENTS
Waking up to discover he is wet can be distressing for your child. Tell him that it's not his fault and reassure him that it's just a phase he'll grow out of.

use the potty in time if he knows you are there to help

● encourage him always to remember to pee before he settles down for the night.

Dealing with accidents

Initially, your child will have accidents at night, especially if you have a boy. This may happen as often as two or three times a week at first, becoming less frequent over the following months, until, by the time he is five, bedwetting is a thing of the past. Until this age, accidents should be seen as natural and unimportant. The best way to deal with them is to:

● stay calm and matter-of-fact—if your child sees that you are upset or worried, it may make him anxious, which could itself affect his ability to control his bladder during the night

● keep a pair of dry pajamas and a spare sheet ready so that you can change your child and the bed with the minimum of fuss

● reassure him that this is a phase that he'll soon grow out of, and he will probably soon become dry.

When he isn't interested

Some children are quite happy to go on wetting their nighttime diapers, especially if their parents don't

❝ George was still wearing a diaper at night when he turned four. I suggested he try a diaperless night and promised him a special treat if he could do it. It took a few nights before his first success, but after a couple of weeks he was dry, and he hasn't had an accident since. ❞

DOROTHY, mother of George, now five

object. Others are afraid of wetting their beds and don't have the confidence to go a night without diapers. If you think your child could manage a dry night, you may need to offer some special motivation.

You could, for example, promise him a special treat for trying. It's important, however, to emphasize the fact that it doesn't matter if the bed does get wet—and that he can always try again the following night. New pajamas or bed linen may help him feel grown-up, but reassure him that everything can be washed so that he doesn't worry too much about ruining his nice new things.

Stress and bedwetting

Sometimes a child who was previously dry may start wetting the bed as a reaction to stress. A number of factors could account for this, including, for example, the arrival of a new baby in the family, moving, or a stay in the hospital.

If it's easy to spot the reasons for the bedwetting, some special attention and lots of reassurance should help—although it may be a little while before it has an effect. If you are unsure of what the problem might be, try talking to your child's teacher or anyone else

HANDY POTTY
Leaving a night-light on and putting a potty by your child's bed will reassure her and help ease her toward dryness at night.

who helps with his care, since they might have a sense of what is bothering your child and how he can be helped.

Later bedwetting

Some children who are over five years of age continue to wet their

beds. In medical terms, this is known as nocturnal (nighttime) enuresis or bedwetting, and it affects about one in six five-year-olds. It's usually boys who are affected, and there is often a family history of bedwetting.

If your child is over five and wets the bed frequently, it may be worth

seeing your doctor to rule out problems such as a urinary tract infection, which can be treated with antibiotics. Usually, however, bedwetting in older children is caused by slow development of the full-bladder response and resolves itself by the time the child is seven years old.

Older children can wear night-time protection pants if they are embarrassed about wearing pullups or diapers. These underpants look and feel like normal underwear but are also absorbent. Children can put them on themselves, which makes them ideal for sleepovers.

Home treatment

There are many things you can do to reassure your child and help him gain nighttime control.

- Tell him that you understand and you know it's not his fault.
- If your child is in the habit of having a bedtime drink, make sure it isn't a large amount of fluid.

WAKING UP TO PEE
If your older child is struggling to gain nighttime control, encouraging him to wake up and use the toilet when you are going to bed may help him along the way.

- Make sure he uses the toilet before settling down for the night.
- Motivate him with small incentives such letting him watch a favorite video when he has a dry night.
- If your child is older, wake him up to pee when you go to bed.

Another measure that can also help is a bedwetting alarm. This is an alarm that goes off each time your child begins to wet the bed, giving him the chance to get up and finish peeing in the toilet. It has been shown to be successful with many children and often works especially well in combination with rewards for dry nights. Talk to your healthcare provider if you think one of these might help.

BEDTIME DRINKS
Having a drink at bedtime should not affect your child's ability to stay dry at night; her bladder's capacity will adjust to the amount of liquid it gets used to.

Questions & Answers

My daughter still drinks a cup of water before going to sleep. Should I stop this to help her stay dry during the night?
It might seem sensible to withhold drinks in the evening as a way of helping your daughter stay dry all night. But you should always let your child drink if she's thirsty—especially since cutting back won't make any difference to her bladder control. If there is less fluid to hold, the bladder adjusts so that it feels as full as it did when it was holding more. And over a period of time, cutting back on drinks will simply reduce the bladder's capacity—

which could make matters worse. Once she has developed enough control to go through the night without wetting the bed, it won't matter how much your daughter drinks—but don't let her have carbonated drinks, drinks with caffeine, or even cow's milk, which contains sugars that can damage a toddler's teeth.

My friend wakes her three-year-old when she goes to bed at night and puts him on the toilet. Is this a good tactic to try?
Many parents do this as a way of avoiding nighttime accidents. But while it helps prevent wet sheets, it doesn't encourage

bladder control. Not only is the child often still half asleep and barely aware of what he is doing, he is also being asked to do the one thing you want to avoid—namely, pee during the night! Instead, you want your child to wake up when he feels the urge to go or hold it until morning. If "lifting" is the only way to prevent accidents, maybe your child isn't developed enough yet to go a whole night without peeing. This tactic might, however, be useful with an older child—one who is five or six and trying hard to keep dry at night. In this case, make sure he is fully awake so he can sense for himself that he has a full bladder.

Potty training guide

Here's a broad guide to the ages and stages of potty training, what you can expect, and what you can do to help your toddler. Remember, as with all developmental milestones, every child will reach the required levels of maturity in his own time.

Baby's age	Your toddler's development	What to expect
up to 18 months	The nerve pathways that connect your baby's bladder and bowel to her brain are not fully matured.	Your baby is still emptying her bowel and bladder automatically as a reflex action, unaware of what is happening.
18 months	The nerve pathways that connect her bladder and bowel to her brain should be fully mature.	Your toddler is starting to develop a degree of control over her bowel and bladder movements—her diapers are often dry for a period of time, and she is becoming aware of what's happening when she pees or poops.
two to three years	As the bladder and bowel muscles strengthen, the ability to "hold it" increases.	Your child is eager to please, wants to imitate you, can follow simple instructions, is reasonably coordinated, and is increasingly anxious to have her independence.
three to five years	Your child's control over her bladder and bowel is sufficient for her to be able to hold it for reasonable periods of time and even wake up at night in response to a full bladder.	Your child is ready to give up diapers at nighttime but, again, expect accidents initially.

What you can do

Start to use words such as "pee" and "poop" when you change her diaper; stay matter-of-fact about dirty diapers, and let her see you and your partner using the toilet.

Introduce your toddler to the potty, but don't expect to start potty training yet.

Start potty training—but don't expect too much too soon. Initially, there may be lots of accidents.

Stay calm and relaxed to increase your child's confidence that she can get it right. With older children, small incentives can often help.

Useful contacts

UNITED STATES

American Academy of Pediatrics
141 Northwest Point Boulevard
Elk Grove Village, IL 60007-1098
(847) 434-4000
General information for parents, as
well as a pediatrician referral service.

The American Medical Association
515 North State Street
Chicago, IL 60610
(800) 621-8335/(312) 464-5000
www.ama-assn.org

Autism Society of America
7910 Woodmont Avenue, Suite 300
Bethesda, MD 20814-3067
(301) 657-0881/(800) 3AUTISM
www.autism-society.org
Information, guidance and support
to families who have a child with
autism.

Baby Center
163 Freelon Street
San Francisco, CA 94107
(866) 241-2229 *(Store Customer Service)*
www.babycenter.com
Information, support and guidance
for parents.

Child Development Institute
3528 E. Ridgeway Road
Orange, CA 92867
(714) 998-8617
Advice and information on potty
training, parenting, and development.

Children's Virtual Hospital
www.vh.org/navigation/vch/topics/p
ediatric_patient_toilet_training_and_be
dwetting.html
Digital health services library
providing information and advice for
toilet training and bedwetting.

KidsHealth
www.kidshealth.org
Information on toilet training and all
areas of children's health.

www.mothheart.com
Advice and links on potty training
and related supplies.

Nation's Network of Children Care Resource and Referral (NACCRAA)
1319 F Street, NW, Suite 500
Washington, DC 20004
(800) 424-2246/(202) 393 5501
www.naccrra.org
www.childcareaware.org
A network of child care resources and
referral centers.

National Dissemination Center for Children with Disabilities
P.O. Box 1492
Washington, DC 20013
(800) 695-0285 v/tty
www.nichcy.org
Information and resources for families
with disabled children.

National Down Syndrome Society
666 Broadway
New York, NY 10012
(212) 460-9330/(800) 221-4602
www.ndss.org
Advice on potty training a child with
Down Syndrome.

National Kidney Foundation National Enuresis Society (NES)
30 East 33rd St., Suite 1100
New York, NY 10016
(800) 622-9010/(212) 889-2210
www.kidney.org/patients/bw/
index.cfm
Information and advice on wetting.

NICHD Information Resource Center (IRC)
P.O. Box 3006
Rockville, MD 20847
(800) 370-2943 (information specialist
hotline)
www.nichd.nih.gov
Information and support on health
issues.

Enuresis Research & Development Center
P.O. Box 2114
Oceanside, CA 92056
(888) 423-3938
www.stopbedwettingfree.com
Information and programs for
bedwetting control.

CANADA

Canadian Parents Online
45 Coulter Avenue
St. Thomas, ON N5R 5A5
(519) 637 7342
www.canadianparents.com
A parent-friendly website with
information on child development,
including potty training.

Canadian Paediatric Society
2204 Walkley Road
Suite 100
Ottawa, ON K1G 4GS
(613) 526-9397
www.cps.ca
Expert advice for parents on child
health and development issues,
including potty training.

Parent Help Line Kids Help Phone National Office
439 University Avenue
Suite 300
Toronto, ON M5G 1Y8
(416) 586-5437
www.parentsinfo.sympatico.ca
Offers parents and caregivers
information, support and referrals
24 hours a day. Includes information
on potty training and bedwetting.

Index

A

accidents 29, 32, 33, 37–41, 44
  bedwetting 55–9
action plans 27–33, 48–9
age
  dryness at night 53, 54,
    57–8, 59, 60–1
  introducing potties 17, 20,
    61
  readiness for training 7, 9,
    11–13, 25, 60–1
alarms, bedwetting 59
asking for the potty 31, 32, 34
awareness 7, 8, 9, 29, 30, 60

B

bedding 53, 55, 56, 57
bedwetting 55–9
bladder control development
  7, 53, 54, 58, 60
bladder emptying, automatic
  7, 31, 53, 60
bottom wiping 33–4
bowel movements
  automatic 7, 31, 45, 60
  constipation & loose
    stools 39, 43, 51
boys 11, 19, 34, 41–3, 51

C

car trips 19, 47–51
clothes 14, 25, 29, 32, 39, 48
  underpants 24, 27, 28, 29,
    58
comments see negative
  comments; praise &
  encouragement
constipation 39, 43, 51
coordination 8, 10, 39

D

daycare & nursery school
  35, 40
daytime naps 33, 37, 38, 39, 53
delaying training 14, 15, 22, 38
development 7–13, 23, 27, 53,
  54, 60

diaper use after training
  starts 29, 33, 45, 50, 53, 54
disposable training pants 29
dressing 25, 32, 39
drinks 32, 35, 43, 47, 50, 58, 59
dryness
  achieving 27–35, 37, 44
  nighttime 37, 53–9, 60–1

E

encouragement see praise &
  encouragement

F

fears 19, 22, 40, 42–3
fluid intake 32, 35, 43, 47, 50,
  58, 59
flushing, fear of 43

G

genetic & family links 7, 57
girls 11, 19, 33–4, 51

H

hand-washing 23, 25
hanging on 7, 31, 51, 53, 60
hygiene 18, 23, 25, 41

I

incentives & rewards 27, 29,
  34–5, 57, 59
independence 9, 11, 17, 23
  lack of 25
inheritance 7, 57
instructions, understanding
  & following 9, 10
interest 8, 24, 25

L

language & vocabulary 10,
  22–3, 34, 61
lids, potties 19, 47
lifting 58, 59
loose stools 39

M

mattress covers 53, 55

N

naps 33, 37, 38, 39, 53
negative comments 10, 11,
  33, 34, 40, 45
nighttime dryness 37, 53–9,
  60–1

O

outings 19, 47–51

P

underpants 24, 27, 28, 29, 58
parents using the toilet 8, 10,
  18, 20, 42
patience 13, 21, 33, 37, 44, 45,
  56
playing with poop 32
potties
  choosing 18–19
  cleaning 18
  compared to toilets 17
  introducing 17–18, 20–1,
    24, 61
  travel potties 47
praise & encouragement 24,
  27, 32, 33, 34
  excessive praise 21, 33
  for "grown-up" behavior
    22, 23
preparation for training 17–25
pressure to perform 11, 22,
  25, 33, 45, 54
public restrooms 49, 50–1
punishment, negative effects
  33, 40, 45

R

readiness for training 7–13,
  25, 27, 60–1
resistance 11, 13, 22, 25, 38
rewards & incentives 27, 29,
  34–5, 57, 59

S

shopping 47–51
siblings 10, 24
  new siblings 11–12, 15, 57

signs, readiness for training
  8–9
skill development 7–13, 23,
  27, 60
sleep see naps; nighttime
  dryness
social pressures 11–12, 44
special-needs children 12
splash guards 19
stain removal 41
standing up to pee, boys 34,
  41–3, 51
stressful events 14–15, 39, 57

T

timing, starting training
  14–15, 38, 60–1
tiredness 38, 39
toilets
  children's seats 19
  compared to potties 17
  parents using 8, 10, 18, 20
  public/away from home
    49, 50–1
  transition to using 40–5
training pants 29
travel 19, 47–51
travel potties 47, 51
twins 13

U

understanding instructions
  9, 10
undressing & dressing 25,
  32, 39
urinary tract infections 41, 58

V

vocabulary & language 10,
  22–3, 34, 61

W

waterproof sheets 53, 55
weather 12, 14–15

Acknowledgments

Dorling Kindersley would like to thank Sally Smallwood and Ruth Jenkinson for the photography, and Sue Bosanko for compiling the index.

Models Rachana and Arianne Shah, David with Maya Bowles, Naginder with Gobind Jahal, Lily Rose Spick, Jo with Jade Sollinger, Thompson family, Isaac Clyne, Ivor with Ruby Baddiel, Thea Collins, Sharon with Marcus Gunn, Paul with Oscar Ford, Aimee Morland, Jenny with Baobao Cao, Nicolette with Marta Comand, Reilly family, Ria Shah, Mark with Sophira Norr, Maureen and Janis Lopatkin with Mia Schindler, Harvey Barron, Lucas Mtfolo, Tom Orchard, Lou-Fong family.

Hair and makeup Victoria Barnes, Louise Heywood, Susie Kennett, Amanda Clarke

Picture researcher Anna Bedewell

Picture librarian Romaine Werblow

Picture credits
Dorling Kindersley would like to thank the following for their kind permission to reproduce their photographs:
14: ImageState/Pictor: Robert Llewellyn; 15: Getty Images: Britt Erlanson.

All other images © Dorling Kindersley.
For further information, see www.dkimages.com